Original title:

Tapered Moons Around the Witch Heap

Author: Linda Leevike

ISBN HARDBACK: 978-1-80562-092-1

ISBN PAPERBACK: 978-1-80563-613-7

Ritual Of Light Beyond Shadows

In the forest deep where the old trees sigh,
Flickering whispers of magic fly.
An ancient spell in the late dusk's glow,
Calls forth the dreams that are lost below.

Wands held high, in a circle they stand,
Bound by the power of nature's hand.
Stars awaken in the velvet sky,
As lanterns dance, and the night winds sigh.

Voices of the past begin to hum,
In harmony, the enchanted come.
With every breath, the shadows retreat,
To the heartbeat of magic, soft and sweet.

The air grows thick with a silvery mist,
As the spirits of light begin to twist.
Over the ground where the shadows creep,
The ritual's promise, a secret to keep.

As dawn approaches, the darkness yields,
The forest awakens with whispered fields.
In the light beyond where the shadows flee,
A world of wonders for all to see.

A Symphony of Starlit Secrets

In the hush of evening's glow,
Whispers dance where shadows grow.
Celestial notes begin to play,
Telling tales of the ancient way.

Glimmers flicker on velvet skies,
Casting spells with watchful eyes.
Every twinkle sings a tune,
Of forgotten dreams and moon.

A breeze carries a gentle sound,
Of secrets lost and magic found.
Underneath the silver light,
Hearts entwined within the night.

Threads of Mystique in the Night Air

In the stillness, shadows creep,
Weaving stories, secrets deep.
Moonlight breathes on cobbled stones,
Echoing the ancient tones.

Mystic threads of twilight spun,
Wrapped in whispers, softly run.
Ethereal laughter fills the breeze,
A tapestry of cosmic keys.

The night unveils its hidden charms,
With every rustle, every calm.
A dance of fate in darkened skies,
Where wonder holds and magic lies.

Flickers of Wild Magic and Moonlight

Stars align in a twinkling row,
As wild magic begins to flow.
With every pulse, the world ignites,
A tapestry of luminous sights.

Whispers swirl through the cool night air,
As enchanting tales linger there.
Moonlight pours like liquid gold,
In the hearts of the brave and bold.

Sparks of laughter, a flickering flame,
Calling forth the childhood name.
In the stillness, dreams take flight,
Guided by the stars so bright.

Whirling Dreams in the Starlit Cauldron

In the cauldron of the night,
Dreams are stirred in silver light.
Whirling visions swirl around,
A cosmic dance without a sound.

Celestial whispers play their part,
Igniting joy within the heart.
Each moment brews a tale untold,
With stardust spilling, bright and bold.

Beneath the shimmering celestial dome,
Every heartbeat calls us home.
In the stillness, magic brews,
Whirling dreams in mystic hues.

Remnants of Elven Lore and Light

In shadows deep where whispers dwell,
Forgotten tales their secrets tell.
With silver leaves and moonlit grace,
Elven spirits find their place.

The flicker of a fading star,
Brings forth memories from afar.
In ancient groves where legends bloom,
Hope weaves light amid the gloom.

By streams of crystal, soft and clear,
Echoes of laughter fill the air.
A tapestry of dreams entwined,
In twilight's arms, the lost we find.

Yet time has dimmed their gentle glow,
As shadows cast, their whispers slow.
But through the night, a spark remains,
In every heart where magic reigns.

Pulses of the Darkened Glade

Beneath the boughs of twisted trees,
Whispers echo on the breeze.
In hidden depths where shadows play,
Darkened glades keep light at bay.

Flickering flames of distant fight,
Dance like phantoms in the night.
The pulse of magic, thick and raw,
Resonates with Nature's law.

Each rustling leaf, a secret shared,
In twilight's hush, the world laid bare.
Amidst the gloom, the heartbeats thrum,
Reminders of what once had come.

From silent knots, the dread takes form,
A shadowed beast, both fierce and warm.
Yet in this dark, a chance may bloom,
A flicker of hope dispelling doom.

Duned Witches and the Orb of Light

The witches of the dunes take flight,
On whispered winds, devices bright.
With cloaks of sand and lunar hue,
They weave their dreams and magic true.

Within their grasp, an orb aglow,
A shining light, a sacred show.
With every chant, the earth responds,
As darkness yields to what it fond.

Reflections in the Darkened Pool

In the stillness of the inky night,
Lies a pool, so deep and bright.
Reflections dance of stars above,
A mirror of the world, of love.

Each ripple breaks the silent air,
Tales of sorrow, joy, and care.
In the depths, lost spirits sigh,
As time drifts slowly, like a cry.

Beneath the surface, shadows wane,
A world unseen, both rich and plain.
In every glance, a story bound,
In waters deep, the truth is found.

The moonlight shimmers on its face,
Gathering dreams in soft embrace.
In every heart, a wish remains,
Reflections echo, doubt sustains.

Echoes of Ether and Enchantment

Whispers dance in twilight's grace,
In shadows where the fairies trace.
A gentle hum, a silver thread,
Entwines the hearts of those who tread.

With every note, a story gleams,
Of ancient woods and silver dreams.
The breeze enchants, the night unfolds,
In secret tales that time beholds.

Beneath the stars, the magic sways,
As laughter lingers in the bays.
The moonlight weaves through leafy seams,
Bright echoes of our woven dreams.

In twilight's grasp, the magic stirs,
As night enfolds with whispered purrs.
Each shimmer holds a lingering song,
Where echoes of the heart belong.

So listen close, let wonders fly,
In realms where visions dare to lie.
For in the dark, where secrets dwell,
Awaits the tales we yearn to tell.

Silvery Phantoms Over Ancient Grounds

Beneath the boughs where shadows twine,
Awake the whispers, soft, divine.
The phantom sighs in silvered glow,
In ancient lands where spirits flow.

With every rustle of the leaves,
Mysteries hide, the heart deceives.
Through crumbling stone and forgotten lore,
The silvery phantoms whisper more.

They dance on paths where starlight weeps,
In echoes where the old earth keeps.
In twilight's embrace, they take their flight,
Over ancient grounds, a ghostly sight.

Through moonlit meadows, they glide and weave,
In secrets that the night believes.
A tapestry of old and dim,
In silver shrouds, their dances brim.

So trace the steps where shadows play,
In silence where the lost may stray.
For in the night, the echoes sing,
Of silvery phantoms, life's soft wing.

Riddles of the Gibbous Night

In phosphor light, the riddles swirl,
As moonbeams flutter, dreams unfurl.
A gibbous glow, a mystic watch,
In shadowed realms, secrets notch.

Each riddle curves like ancient vines,
Entwined in thoughts of grand designs.
What lies beyond the veil of time,
In moonlit whispers, sweet and prime?

With every tick of midnight's chime,
The questions dance, a rhythmic rhyme.
In spaces deep, where no one goes,
The gibbous night its wisdom shows.

So tread the path where shadows creep,
In riddled dreams, the heart will leap.
For in the stillness, truth ignites,
In silvered folds of gibbous nights.

Let echoes drift on whispered wings,
As starlit riddles weave their strings.
In moon's embrace, we seek and find,
The riddles of the gibbous mind.

Vehement Brews and Moonlit Spells

With cauldrons bubbling, dark and deep,
Old essays filled with secrets keep.
The moonlight spills its silver hue,
As whispers weave through shadowed brew.

A dash of stardust, pinch of sky,
The scents of magic float nearby.
In swirling mists, the potions churn,
As ancient lores in moments burn.

Vehement brews, with powers vast,
In moonlit spells, the die is cast.
The night ignites with fervent cries,
As wishes twinkle in the skies.

Each herb and root, a tale unfolds,
Of courage found and truths retold.
In darkened woods, where spirits dwell,
We craft our fate through mystic spell.

So gather round, let candles flare,
In laughter's joy, we breathe the air.
For in this night of moonlit thrills,
We find our dreams in potent spills.

Shadows Lurking in the Witches' Hollow

In the hollow where whispers creep,
Shadows dance while secrets seep.
Moonlight flickers on ancient trees,
Drawing forth the chilly breeze.

Gnarled roots twist, entwined with fate,
Casting spells that tempt the late.
Magic hums through bramble and thorn,
With every heartbeat, a world reborn.

In hidden corners, phantoms play,
Lingering where the lost souls sway.
A cauldron bubbles with dreams untold,
Enigmas wrapped in silence, bold.

Echoes of laughter mix with dread,
As ancient riddles guide the dead.
Nature's song, both sweet and stark,
Calls forth shadows from the dark.

Serpents of the Starlit Forest

Beneath the glance of twinkling lights,
Serpents slither through the nights.
Whispers slink through rustling leaves,
Carrying tales that night believes.

Cool earth cradles their secrets near,
In shadows thick with ancient fear.
Their scales shimmer with a silent glow,
A warning carried by the breeze that flows.

To venture deep, where few have roamed,
Is to embrace the unknown that's homed.
Glimmers of magic flit and tease,
Among the curling limbs of trees.

In every rustle, a primal call,
A spell woven through the nightfall.
With every breath, mysteries weave,
In the heart of the forest, dreams believe.

Rituals Beneath the Obsidian Vault

Under a sky of obsidian hue,
Rituals stir in shadows few.
Candles flicker with an eerie light,
Marking the edge of day and night.

Figures cloaked in the night's embrace,
Gathered together, a haunting grace.
Chanting words of power and might,
Binding spirits to the site.

While echoes of laughter break the dawn,
Invisible threads in darkness drawn.
Sacred circles carved in stone,
Capturing more than mere flesh and bone.

Spectres in the Veil of Twilight

As twilight falls, the spectres stir,
Along the path, memories blur.
Figures drift with whispers low,
In shadows where the lost ones go.

Through misty veils, their stories glide,
Haunted truths that time can't bide.
With every step, they weave and wind,
A tapestry of the undefined.

In spectral glow, they call your name,
Remnants of love, loss, and fame.
A dance of dreams in shades of grey,
Guiding souls who've lost their way.

Hold fast your heart, confront the dark,
For in the depth lies the spark.
With twilight's end, a new tale spun,
Among the spirits, we become one.

Hallowed Ground Under Starlit Glimmers

In silence whispering secrets deep,
The ancient stones where shadows creep,
Beneath the stars that twinkle bright,
We wander softly through the night.

A dance of moonbeams on the grass,
Where time stands still and moments pass,
In hallowed ground with dreams unfurled,
A tale of magic, softly swirled.

With eyes aglow, we seek the past,
Through echoes of a spell that's cast,
A tapestry of light and lore,
We tread upon that sacred floor.

Whispers of longing fill the air,
As we remember those who dare,
To weave the night with threads of gold,
In hallowed ground, their stories told.

So here we stand with hearts entwined,
In unity with ages lined,
Under the glimmer of starlit skies,
In this enchanted space, we rise.

The Echoes of Spellbound Mornings

Awake beneath the breath of dawn,
The world anew, a hopeful song,
With every hue that paints the day,
The magic stirs, then finds its way.

In golden rays that softly kiss,
Each moment holds a hint of bliss,
A shimmer in the dewdrop's light,
The promise of a day so bright.

With hearts that dance on gentle breeze,
We chase the whispers through the trees,
The echoes of the night still near,
In spellbound mornings, crystal clear.

Birds take flight on wings of hope,
As dreams awaken, learn to cope,
The sky above—a canvas wide,
Where possibilities reside.

So let the sunbeam guide our quest,
With every heartbeat, every breath,
In the embrace of morning light,
We find our path in pure delight.

Constellations Shrouded in Legend

The night unveils its hidden tales,
In constellations, ancient trails,
Stories woven in celestial thread,
Each star a whisper from the dead.

With every flicker, secrets sigh,
The myths arise, they never die,
Of wizards bold and dragons fierce,
In starlit depth, their hearts we pierce.

A journey mapped in cosmic light,
Guides us through the velvet night,
Where legends linger, bold and grand,
In timeless realms, we take a stand.

As shadows dance and spirits play,
We lose ourselves, then find our way,
In constellations, truth enshrined,
With every gaze, a spark entwined.

So let us twirl with stardust grace,
And carve our names in ink of space,
For in the tales of ages past,
The echoes of our dreams will last.

Currents of Enchantment from Above

Above us flow the whispered dreams,
In currents bright, where starlight beams,
A dance of magic in the air,
Inviting hearts to trespass there.

With every breeze, enchantments thrive,
The pulse of life, we feel alive,
Through hidden pathways, soft and clear,
The universe feels ever near.

In silver threads of twilight's weave,
We find the strength to dare believe,
That every moment holds the key,
To mysteries we yearn to see.

The secrets carried by the night,
In currents swift, they take their flight,
A tapestry of shadowed lore,
Awaits the hearts that seek to soar.

So trust the winds, let spirits roam,
In currents of enchantment, home,
With soul set free, we'll journey wide,
In stellar realms, forever tied.

Ethereal Beckonings from the Grove

In shadows thick where willows sway,
The whispered winds begin to play.
Soft glimmers dance, a subtle light,
As nature's secrets weave from night.

Beneath the boughs, the spirits hum,
A melody where dreams now come.
The ancient trees, they softly sigh,
Inviting all who wander by.

In twilight's grasp, a portal gleams,
Where fairy tales blend with our dreams.
Each rustle speaks, each starry gleam,
Awakening the heart to dream.

The mossy floor holds stories old,
Of love and loss, of heroes bold.
In every root and every stone,
The past is whispered, never alone.

So heed the call from deep within,
Let the magic of the grove begin.
For in its heart where shadows play,
Ethereal beckonings guide our way.

Nocturnal Rituals in the Undergrowth

When midnight cloaks the forest floor,
A dance unfolds, a silent roar.
The moonlight spills like silver dust,
In shadows deep where secrets trust.

Small creatures scurry, shadows flit,
With nature's rhythm, they perfectly fit.
A circle forms beneath the trees,
In whispered vows, the night's gentle breeze.

Old patterns rise in sacred space,
To conjure dreams, to trace their grace.
A luminescent glow, a spell,
In undergrowth where mysteries dwell.

Each fungus glows with ancient lore,
As twinkling lights begin to soar.
An owl's call breaks the tender hush,
And echoes through the midnight rush.

In nocturnal rites, the past ignites,
With every heart that stirs in nights.
The forest sighs, a knowing sigh,
In rituals where spirits lie.

Glimmers of the Arcane Above

Amidst the stars, a soft refrain,
Glimmers of magic lie not in vain.
With every twinkle, secrets bloom,
In the vastness of night's dark room.

Celestial trails of silver lace,
Illuminate time and sacred space.
The constellations weave their tales,
Of ancient wizards and their gales.

With every wish cast on the night,
A glimmer speaks, a gentle light.
The cosmos hums a lullaby,
As echoes of eternity sigh.

In the whispers of the heavens high,
The arcane dances, never shy.
Each star a promise, each moonlit glow,
A beacon of love for souls that know.

So gaze up high, let hearts align,
With glimmers bright, the stars entwine.
In night's embrace, magic awaits,
With open hearts, we dance with fates.

Folklore Whispers Beneath the Night Sky

In shadows deep where echoes dwell,
Folklore whispers, casting spells.
Tales of old in twilight's fold,
Of brave young hearts and legends bold.

Beneath the sky, where dreams entwine,
Fables linger like aged wine.
As stories weave through rustling leaves,
The night unveils what one believes.

From ancient script to whispered air,
Every glance a story to share.
The crickets sing a melody sweet,
As magic pulses beneath our feet.

In every shadow, a tale is spun,
Of battles fought and battles won.
With every breeze, a memory spins,
In folklore's grasp, where life begins.

So gather close, let hearts unite,
To share the whispers of the night.
In tales and dreams, we find our way,
And weave the magic of today.

Wisdom Woven in Silver Threads

In the quiet of the night, so deep,
Whispers of ancient secrets creep.
With threads of silver spun so fine,
Wisdom glimmers in the moonshine.

Books unfurl their tales so vast,
Lessons learned from ages past.
Like stars that guide the lost at sea,
Echoes of knowledge set us free.

Underneath the watchful gaze,
Lies the charm of forgotten days.
In every word, a story grows,
In every heart, the magic flows.

Through misty woods where shadows play,
Elders speak what they can't relay.
In the light, their voices blend,
Woven wisdom, the eternal friend.

As dawn arrives with gentle sighs,
The silver threads in daylight rise.
Embrace the truth, let it unfurl,
In every heart, a shining pearl.

Echoing Voices of the Witching Hour

As moonlight bathes the world in grace,
Echoing voices begin to trace.
Secrets whispered on the breeze,
Stirring dreams from slumber's ease.

Witches dance in shadows' embrace,
With laughter soft, they find their place.
In circles formed by glowing fire,
They conjure spells that never tire.

Silver owls on silent wings,
Carry tales that midnight brings.
From thickets green to starlit skies,
The witching hour reveals their ties.

Every rustle, every sigh,
Bears witness to the nighttime cry.
Mystic creatures weave and roam,
In the heart, they find their home.

When dawn arrives, the shadows fade,
Yet, in our hearts, the magic stayed.
Echoes linger, forever near,
Whispers of the night we hold dear.

Silken Tides of the Celestial Sea

Beneath the stars, so bright and bold,
The celestial sea's secrets unfold.
Silken tides of shimmering light,
Kiss the shores of the endless night.

Waves that shimmer with silver gleam,
Carry the weight of every dream.
In currents deep, the wishes glide,
Held in the arms of the moon's tide.

As constellations softly sway,
Guiding lost souls who drift away.
In the stillness, a lullaby,
Cradled in whispers from the sky.

The ocean's heart beats strong and true,
Reflecting the heavens' endless blue.
With every wave, the cosmos speaks,
In tranquil tones, through mystic peaks.

And when the dawn breaks through the haze,
The magic wanes, yet still it stays.
In every heart, the sea's embrace,
Waves of wonder, life's sacred grace.

Crescents and Chimeras Under Dark Canopies

Beneath the arch of twilight's veil,
Crescents bright whisper a tale.
In shadows' fold, chimeras play,
Dancing in dreams that drift away.

With fleeting forms of mist and light,
They twirl beneath the cloak of night.
Dark canopies of emerald trees,
Sing soft songs with every breeze.

In glades where secrets intertwine,
Magic breathes, pure and divine.
Eyes aglow with stories spun,
In the heart, the night has won.

Through corridors of starlit skies,
The echoes of ancient lullabies.
Crescents gleam and shadows leap,
Guarding the dreams that we keep.

As dawn emerges, the shadows fade,
Yet in their wake, memories stayed.
Crescents and chimeras, forever free,
Woven in the night's tapestry.

Chilling Whispers on Dewy Ferns

In the glade where silence dwells,
Chilling whispers cast their spells.
Dewy ferns in moonlit grace,
Gather secrets, time won't erase.

Ghostly winds weave through the trees,
Softly rustling leaves, a tease.
Misty breaths of ancient lore,
Haunting echoes from the shore.

Footsteps tread on soil so light,
Muffled under the silver night.
Creatures linger, spirits roam,
In this quiet, wild home.

Stars above, a watchful eye,
Glimmer softly like a sigh.
Night unfolds its velvet shroud,
Beneath starlit, silver cloud.

Whispers still beneath the fronds,
Dreams and darkness play their bonds.
In the hush where shadows spin,
Chilling whispers draw us in.

Skylarks in the Ebon Field

Skylarks rise in ebon skies,
Singing songs of hidden ties.
Between the fields, a dance of light,
Chasing shadows through the night.

Windswept grass, a gentle sway,
Echoes of a fleeting day.
Beneath the stars, hearts align,
In the dark, their voices shine.

Moonlit paths where starlight trails,
Softly whispering feathered tales.
Ebon fields embrace the near,
As skylarks weave their melodies clear.

Horizon spills with colors bold,
Stories of the brave retold.
Each note dances on the breeze,
Carrying with it, sweet esprit.

In the stillness, dreams take flight,
With the skylarks through the night.
Together they will find the way,
As dawn will chase the shadows away.

The Luminous Curse of Solstice Night

On solstice night, when shadows creep,
A luminous curse begins to leap.
Bright orbs of light, they softly glow,
In the woods where wildflowers grow.

Beware the glow that beckons near,
A haunting song, a whispered cheer.
For under starlit celestial frames,
Lies a tapestry of whispered names.

Veils of mist weave through the trees,
Carrying secrets on the breeze.
Those who linger feel the pull,
Of the night, both dark and full.

Through the woods, the shadows spin,
Drawn to paths where dreams begin.
The curse of light, a lure so sweet,
Carries hearts to their solemn beat.

Yet amidst the lure of the night,
Lies a truth shrouded in fright.
To dance with shadows, heed the call,
For in the end, we risk it all.

Shadows Twisting Around the Hollow Fire

By the hollow fire's flickering glow,
Shadows twist in a rhythmic flow.
Ancient stories whispered low,
As embers drift like timeless snow.

The air is thick with echoes past,
Haunting whispers that hold us fast.
Around the flames, the darkness sings,
Of forgotten tales and spectral things.

Faces dance in the orange light,
Chasing shadows through the night.
Every flicker tells a tale,
Of lives entwined where spirits wail.

Beneath the stars, a secret pact,
With shadows that will not retract.
Around the fire, we share our fears,
With shadows that have seen our tears.

As the fire wanes, the night grows bold,
And weaves a tapestry of old.
We learn that shadows always stay,
Even as the flames fade away.

Twilight Serenade of the Arcane

In twilight's gentle, woven thread,
Whispers float where shadows tread.
Ancient trees with secrets hold,
Stories of the wise and bold.

Stars awaken, dreams collide,
Magic swirls, no place to hide.
With every glance, the night reveals,
The heart's desires, and how it feels.

The moonlight dances, soft and bright,
Guiding lost souls through the night.
A haunting lullaby takes flight,
In the stillness, hearts unite.

Figures cloaked in silver glow,
In the dark where no one goes.
Their secrets carried on the breeze,
A melody that stirs the trees.

As stars align, a spell is cast,
Binding futures to the past.
Twilight's magic, vast and wide,
Calls to those who've lost their guide.

Silhouettes Dancing in the Mist

In the cool embrace of dawn's first light,
Silhouettes swirl, a ghostly sight.
Through the fog, they come alive,
In the dance where shadows thrive.

Mist wraps 'round with whispered sighs,
Enchantments weave beneath the skies.
Each step a tale of love and loss,
In the silence, the world bears the cross.

Amidst the trees that sway and bend,
The fleeting figures twist and blend.
Every movement, a promise made,
In the heart of the twilight shade.

Time stands still, the night extends,
While the dance of secrets wends.
Through the haze, lost voices call,
In this world, we rise and fall.

With every twirl, the echoes play,
A haunting song at break of day.
Silhouettes fade as light ascends,
Leaving dreams that time suspends.

Nightfall's Embrace on Ancient Stones

On ancient stones, where history sleeps,
Nightfall embraces, a secret keeps.
Echoes murmur through the air,
In the silence, shadows snare.

The stars ignite with stories old,
A tapestry of dreams retold.
Beneath the vault of endless night,
Whispers linger, soft and light.

Candles flicker in hidden nooks,
Casting spells like storybooks.
The air is thick with time's embrace,
In this sacred, tranquil space.

Each stone a witness to the past,
Guarding secrets, shadows cast.
Nightfall weaves its gentle seam,
Embracing all within a dream.

As dawn approaches, soft and true,
The stones still sing of me and you.
In the light, the shadows wane,
Yet in the heart, they still remain.

Enigma of the Lunar Whisper

Under the moon's soft, silver gaze,
Mysteries swirl in a glowing haze.
Whispers beckon from the deep,
In secrets held that night shall keep.

The stars above, bright beacons shine,
Carving paths where souls entwine.
In every sigh, a promise sways,
As the night whispers its ancient ways.

Lunar shadows dance with grace,
Guiding dreams to a secret place.
Through the dark, where echoes flow,
The heart unveils what time may know.

A gentle pull, an unseen thread,
Draws the living from the dead.
In realms where whispers softly play,
A harmony that leads astray.

The enigma of the night unfolds,
Crafting tales that time beholds.
In every breath, the lunar kiss,
Awakens magic in the abyss.

Whispers in the Crescent Night

In moonlit glades where secrets sigh,
The silver beams weave dreams that fly.
Soft whispers brush the slumbering trees,
As night unfolds on gentle breeze.

Stars glimmer like forgotten lore,
Each twinkle holds a tale of yore.
The owls call in cryptic tones,
While shadows wrap the ancient stones.

Misty trails in silence flow,
Guiding hearts where few dare go.
The crescent moon, a guiding hand,
In realms where fantasy does stand.

With every step, the magic swells,
In secret paths where twilight dwells.
A tapestry of night so bright,
Awakens souls to pure delight.

So linger here in serenade,
Where time and space are softly played.
For in the whispers, truth ignites,
In the embrace of crescent nights.

Shadows Danced on Embered Stone

Beneath the stars, the shadows twine,
On embered stones, their steps align.
A flickering glow from fires' heart,
Where tales of old begin to start.

With every crackle, secrets shared,
The night reveals what once was dared.
Dancing forms in twilight's grace,
As echoes fill this hallowed space.

The air is thick with whispered dreams,
A symphony of moonlit themes.
Each movement paints the twilight air,
A sight that stirs a longing flare.

They sway and twist, a spectral view,
In garments spun from night's own hue.
Each shadow holds a tale to weave,
In every pulse, they'll never leave.

So watch and listen, let it flow,
For in their dance, the magic grows.
On embered stones where shadows play,
Timeless whispers softly sway.

Lunar Veils Beneath the Lichen

In twilight's hush, a veil is cast,
Where time and space meet shadows vast.
With every breath, the lichen glows,
The secrets that the forest knows.

The moon drapes softly on the ground,
In silver threads, a world unbound.
Nature hums a lullaby sweet,
As mysteries beneath it meet.

Beneath the blooms and tangled roots,
The earth holds tales in subtle flutes.
A realm where love and magic blend,
With every whisper, the way extends.

So wander forth, your heart aflame,
Where spirits dance, and none feel shame.
For in the night, the veils unfold,
A story waiting to be told.

With every step on moonlit trail,
You'll find the truth in every tale.
Embrace the magic, hold it tight,
As lunar veils weave through the night.

The Enchantment of Fading Light

As daylight bows to night's embrace,
The sky transforms, a softer space.
With whispered sighs and fading hues,
The world is clad in evening's blues.

The sun dips low, its fire spent,
While stars awake, their twinkles lent.
A gentle breeze, the nightbird's call,
Invites the dreams, enchanting all.

Fragrant blooms release their sweet,
As darkness drapes the earth's retreat.
In twilight's glow, the secrets bloom,
A realm anew, where shadows loom.

The softening light, a tender touch,
With every heartbeat, meant so much.
It holds the whispers of the night,
Wrapping you tight in purest light.

So cherish this enchanted phase,
Where fading light begins to graze.
For in its grasp, the world feels right,
An invitation to the night.

Secrets in the Silvered Glow

In twilight's hush, secrets unfurl,
Whispers dance in a lonesome swirl.
Beneath the stars, shadows take flight,
Guarding dreams through the velvet night.

Moonbeams weave with silver thread,
Painting tales of the long since dead.
Softly calling, the heartbeats sigh,
Hidden truths that in silence lie.

A rustling breeze through the ancient trees,
Carrying echoes of long-lost pleas.
Flickering starlight, a beckoning lure,
In the silvered glow, we find what's pure.

Glimmering orbs on a darkened stream,
Lending the world a mystical dream.
Each shimmer tells of the paths we tread,
Leading us back to the things unsaid.

In corners where the shadows loom,
Awaits the spark with a hint of gloom.
Secrets linger where the heartbeats quick,
In the silvered glow, they bind and stick.

Echoes of the Fog-kissed Night

In the quiet where shadows creep,
Fog blankets dreams lost in deep.
Voices murmur, a soft refrain,
Carrying tales of forgotten pain.

The lanterns flicker, casting glow,
Guiding lost hearts where few dare go.
Through the mist whispers the night,
Sheltering secrets from the light.

Each step echoes on cobblestone,
Tracing paths of the long-time gone.
The air thick with stories untold,
Of love and loss, of the brave and bold.

As the moon wears her misty crown,
The world outside slips further down.
In the fog, creatures softly sway,
Dancing with shadows till break of day.

Yet beneath this eerie, gentle veil,
Lies a magic that cannot fail.
For in every breath and sigh tonight,
Echoes the heartbeat of dark delight.

The Witch's Lanterns in Dusk's Embrace

In dusky light, the lanterns sway,
A beacon for souls who lose their way.
With flickering flames in colors bright,
They guide the lost through the fading night.

Mysterious glow from the spellbound trees,
Weaves tales as old as the evening breeze.
With each whisper, secrets ignite,
In the realm where shadows take flight.

In the cauldron, the potion brews,
A tapestry woven with vivid hues.
Starlit visions and mystical charms,
Holding the world in bewitching arms.

When dusk descends with a gentle sigh,
And the moon ascends to the haunted sky,
The witch in her cloak blends in with peace,
Illuminating love that will never cease.

So step lightly in this enchanted space,
For secrets linger in every trace.
Each twinkle and glimmer, a promise remains,
In the witch's lanterns, hope sustains.

Glistening Orbs of the Haunted Sky

Above the trees, in the midnight glow,
Glistening orbs in the haunted flow.
They whisper tales of the lost and found,
In the silence of night, a timeless sound.

The stars conjure wishes, soft as dew,
Crafting dreams with a shimmer anew.
Each light a beacon for those adrift,
Carrying hope in the dark, a gift.

As shadows lengthen, the air turns cold,
Spectres dance where the stories unfold.
With every flicker, a spirit's sigh,
Glistening orbs paint the night sky.

In this realm where the wraiths take flight,
Echoing whispers take grasp of the night.
Their tales entwined in a tapestry spun,
Binding the lost till the night is done.

So look to the heavens, where magic resides,
In glistening orbs where the mystery hides.
For in each twinkle, a spark of delight,
Awakens the heart to the wonders of night.

Fragments of Forgotten Galaxies

Stars once bright, now whispers low,
Drift through shadows, time's soft glow.
A cosmic dance of lost embrace,
Echoes linger in empty space.

Fragments swirling in silent storms,
Memories wrapped in celestial forms.
Galaxies fade, yet dreams remain,
A tapestry woven in starlit pain.

Wonders hidden in twilight's shroud,
Ghostly tales sung soft, yet loud.
Nebulas bloom in quiet sighs,
As the universe breathes and dies.

Whispers of light in velvet deep,
New worlds stir from ancient sleep.
Through the void, faint hopes ignite,
In the heart of an endless night.

Fragments shimmer, the past calls clear,
Timeless truths in the void we hear.
A journey through the vast unknown,
In the cosmos, we are not alone.

Harmony of the Gloaming Singers

In the twilight, voices blend,
Nature's hymn as day must end.
Crickets chirp, a soft refrain,
Melodies woven, joy and pain.

Beneath the stars, a chorus sweet,
Echoes rise where forest meets.
Whispering winds through branches play,
Guide the heart as night holds sway.

Moonlit rays on silver streams,
Companions of our deepest dreams.
Singers' souls in harmony,
Carving paths through history.

Stillness wraps the world in grace,
Each note finds its rightful place.
Together bound, through life we roam,
In nature's arms, we are home.

The gloaming calls, soft secrets spun,
A melody at dusk begun.
Heartfelt echoes blend and soar,
In harmony, forevermore.

Visions Beneath a Veil of Silver

Beneath the moon's soft silver cloak,
Whispers weave through dreams bespoke.
Visions dance on shimmering light,
Guided by the stars at night.

Secrets deep as ocean's sigh,
Linger softly, drift and fly.
In the stillness, shadows play,
Mysteries of the night turn day.

Glimmers echo through time's embrace,
Timeless wonders in empty space.
Each heartbeat sings of stories told,
Within the silver, visions bold.

Lost in reveries, we wander far,
Chasing dreams, each wish a scar.
Beneath the veil, truths intertwine,
In the fabric of the divine.

Visions fade like morning dew,
Yet linger sweet in hearts so true.
A tapestry of night's allure,
In every moment, we endure.

Witches' Brew in the Dim Glow

In cauldrons deep, the secrets swirl,
Herbs and shadows dance and twirl.
A pinch of stardust, a moonlit sigh,
Woven spells in the night sky.

Fingers trace the ancient runes,
Whispered curses, forgotten tunes.
Gloaming's magic, a sacred rite,
Awakens spirits of the night.

Beneath the boughs, the potions brew,
The air aglow with every hue.
Laughter mingles with the smoke,
Each incantation softly spoke.

To bind the past, to dream the new,
In every glance, a world askew.
Witching hour, a fleeting chance,
To weave our fate in the evening dance.

Dim light flickers, the circle gleams,
A tapestry of woven dreams.
In witches' brew, our hearts align,
Magic lives where the stars entwine.

Echoes of Secrets in the Dark

In shadows deep where whispers creep,
The secrets stir, a quiet keep.
Beneath the moon's soft silver gaze,
Flicker the truths of forgotten days.

Old trees hum with voices lost,
Their tales untold, yet at a cost.
Boys in cloaks, with eyes aglow,
Chase fleeting dreams where shadows flow.

A crystal orb in twilight's hand,
Holds memories of a bygone land.
The murmurs rise like misty air,
Carrying stories of joy and despair.

From cracks in stone, the phantoms rise,
A haunting song 'neath starlit skies.
With every beat, the heartbeats call,
Invoking magic beyond the wall.

In this realm where echoes dwell,
The darkest secrets weave a spell.
With bated breath, await the dawn,
A world awakened, shadows drawn.

Celestial Charms in a Witch's Glade

In the heart of woods, where fairies wink,
Weave spells with laughter, unbroken link.
Moonlight dances on the dew-kissed leaves,
Crafting charms that the night receives.

Ancient stones hum with power bold,
Guarding secrets the glade has told.
A cauldron bubbles with herbs and lore,
Brewing dreams that the wildflowers adore.

The air is thick with scents so sweet,
Ginger and honey, a fragrant treat.
Wands twirl gently, a flick and sigh,
As constellations twinkle high.

With every chant, the stars align,
Binding magic, a thread divine.
The whispers of nature, soft yet clear,
Guide the hearts of those who dare near.

So linger here where the spirits play,
In the witch's glade, by night and day.
For every charm and dream that's spun,
Holds the promise of a life begun.

Silvered Spheres Amongst the Pines

Beneath the boughs of ancient trees,
Silvered spheres twirl on the breeze.
Laughter echoes, soft and bright,
As echoes of joy fill the night.

Gentle winds carry tales from far,
Of lost loves and wished-upon stars.
With every glimmer, a story unfolds,
Whispering secrets in stardust molds.

Pinecones scatter, a nature's art,
With every heartbeat, magic starts.
A world alive with shimmering dreams,
Each silver orb a promise gleams.

Moonlit pathways guide the way,
To hidden places where shadows play.
Drawn by the pull of celestial light,
Adventures wait in the soft twilight.

As dawn approaches, the light ascends,
The silvered spheres, their journey bends.
In nature's cradle, timeless and free,
Awaits a magic only we can see.

The Cauldron's Glow at Twilight's Edge

At twilight's edge, the cauldron glows,
With bubbles rising in mystic flows.
A potion stirs, rich and rare,
Catch a glimpse, if you dare.

Frothy brews of candy dreams,
Infused with echoes and laughter's themes.
Murmurs dance as shadows play,
In this enchanted end of day.

The air is thick with tales untold,
Of daring deeds and hearts so bold.
With fire's warmth and flickering light,
Magic whispers through the night.

Wands drawn forth, the spell is cast,
Entwining futures with echoes past.
The simmering pot sings a tune,
Of wishes granted beneath the moon.

So gather close, let spirits flow,
In the cauldron's glow, let secrets show.
At twilight's edge, let your heart ignite,
As dreams unfold beneath starlit night.

Influence of the Strange and Shining

In twilight whispers, shadows dance,
A glow ignites, as dreams entrance.
With every flicker, stories weave,
The strange and shining, we believe.

Across the night, the stars align,
Casting spells, a fate divine.
In their brilliance, hearts will soar,
Embracing magic, evermore.

Each shimmering light, a tale untold,
Of daring paths and courage bold.
The moonlit whispers call us near,
To seek the wonders, hold them dear.

Mysteries flicker in silver streams,
Awakening our deepest dreams.
The strange, a fire, ignites the night,
In magical worlds, we take flight.

So let us wander, hand in hand,
Through realms where time cannot withstand.
In this influence, we will find,
The strange and shining, intertwined.

Secrets of the Pendulum Moon

When midnight chimes, the secrets pour,
From pendulum swings and ancient lore.
Echoes linger, soft and low,
Where shadows twist and secrets grow.

A dance of time, it sways and turns,
Revealing all that brightly burns.
In every tick, a story calls,
The pendulum swings while evening falls.

Whispers wrap around the night,
In moonlit paths, obscured from sight.
With every swing, we dare to seek,
The truths that linger, strange yet sleek.

Modes of fate reflect in glass,
Tender moments, fleeting, pass.
Yet in the stillness, hearts will yearn,
For secrets kept and lessons learned.

The pendulum pauses, then takes flight,
In cycles deep, fades to twilight.
As shadows fade, and silence falls,
The secrets linger in starlit halls.

Elusive Forms Beneath a Shrouded Sky

Beneath the shroud, lost forms await,
In whispered breaths, they circulate.
Imagination leads us on,
Through veiled realms where light has shone.

Each fleeting shape, a wisp of dreams,
Emerging softly from the seams.
They beckon close, yet slip away,
Elusive forms that long to stay.

Through foggy paths, they twist and glide,
In shadow's depths, their secrets hide.
With every glance, a fleeting trace,
Awakens hope in boundless space.

The morning sun may chase them here,
But hidden still, they reappear.
In shimmering folds and playful hues,
We find the life that we can choose.

So let us wander, eyes aglow,
In search of forms that ebb and flow.
In twilight's clasp, we find our way,
Through shrouded skies, come what may.

Glances at Eternities in the Dark

In quiet moments, darkness blooms,
Reflecting thoughts in silent rooms.
Eternities whisper, softly sigh,
In shadows deep, where secrets lie.

The stars above, mere pinpricks bright,
Guide our hearts through endless night.
Each glance reveals a flicker of fate,
As timeless magic weaves and waits.

Mysteries linger, folded tight,
In depths unseen by mortal sight.
The clock ticks on, yet still we fall,
Into the depths of night's sweet call.

With hearts alight, we take our stand,
To chase the dreams that fate has planned.
In the dark, we find our spark,
With glances cast at time's embrace.

So let us wander through this maze,
In search of light amidst the haze.
For in the dark, the truth ignites,
With glances at what time unites.

Shadows Weave a Tale Untold

In corners dim where whispers dwell,
The shadows dance, a timeless spell.
They weave a tale from dusk till dawn,
Of secrets kept and hope reborn.

Through silken threads of ancient strife,
They chase the dreams of fleeting life.
In every flicker, stories flow,
From hearth to heart, where embers glow.

The night unfolds its velvet hand,
As shadows draw the dreams we planned.
With every sigh, a truth concealed,
In quiet realms, our fate revealed.

Yet laughter lingers, soft and bright,
In shadows cast by starry light.
With every step, a voice will surge,
In twilight's arms, the worlds converge.

So let the shadows gently weave,
The tales of those who choose to believe.
For in the dark, we learn to see,
The stories that set our spirits free.

Dreams Intertwined with Celestial Dust

Beneath the glow of countless stars,
We weave our wishes, near and far.
With every dream, a sigh takes flight,
On wings of hope, through endless night.

Celestial dust upon our skin,
A touch of magic buried within.
In realms where slumber holds its reign,
We dance along the stardust lane.

With every heartbeat, stories blend,
As galaxies twist and worlds extend.
In whispered breaths, our futures gleam,
In every pulse, the promise of a dream.

Awake we rise to face the dawn,
Yet shadows of our dreams carry on.
The cosmos wraps us in its prose,
In silken threads, our hearts compose.

And so we wander, hand in hand,
Through twisted paths of a stardust land.
For in our dreams, we find our place,
In celestial dust, we leave a trace.

The Circle's Embrace at Day's End

The sun bows low, the shadows blend,
In twilight's hush, where timers bend.
A circle forms, both soft and round,
With laughter echoing all around.

In whispered tales, the day's refrain,
We join our hearts in joy and pain.
As dusk enfolds, we share our light,
In the circle's arms, we unite.

Each story shared, a spark ignites,
In glowing embers that paint the nights.
We breathe together, the moment shared,
In this embrace, we hold the dared.

The moon ascends to claim its throne,
While stars applaud our dreams well-known.
A circle of souls, an endless quest,
In twilight's arms, forever blessed.

So hold my hand as shadows sway,
And let us dance till break of day.
For in this moment, we shall find,
The circle's love, forever kind.

Enigmas of the Night-Blooming Flora

In gardens veiled by evening's breath,
Where secrets bloom and silence rests.
The night unfolds its fragrant lace,
With petals soft in dark embrace.

Each flower tells a tale untold,
Of mysteries quiet, fierce, and bold.
As moonlight weaves through leaves so green,
The whispers dance in shadows seen.

Night-blooming flora, shy and rare,
Release their scent into the air.
In this dark haven, magic thrives,
Where every flower's spirit strives.

With twinkling stars as guiding lights,
We wander through enchanted nights.
In every shade, a story spun,
Where dreams take wing and hearts are won.

So pause awhile in nature's thrall,
To witness beauty's tender call.
For in the night, in every bloom,
Lie enigmas that dispel the gloom.

Whispers of the Celestial Dust

In the hush of twilight's breath,
Stars awaken from their rest,
Casting dreams on silver paths,
Where wishes weave their gentle quest.

Through the veil of velvet night,
Echoes shimmer, soft and bright,
Voices of the cosmos sing,
Tales of magic, love, and light.

The moon whispers secrets deep,
In shadows where the stardust sweeps,
Floating on a cosmic breeze,
Nature's lullaby, a heart that leaps.

In gardens where the night blooms thrice,
Celestial boughs in twinkling guise,
Each petal sings a song of old,
A tapestry of cosmic ties.

Glimmers twine with dreams unspun,
A realm where time and space are one,
With each whisper, fate and chance,
In the dance of stars, we run.

Shadows of the Enchanted Cradle

In corners dark, where secrets lie,
A cradle rocks 'neath starlit sky,
Whispers of lore, both soft and sweet,
Guard dreams that dance and flutter by.

The shadows weave a tale so grand,
Of ancient woods, and far-off lands,
Where twilight mingles with the dawn,
And magic slips through gentle hands.

Muffled giggles fill the air,
As night unfolds its silken hair,
Through golden threads of moonlight spun,
In the cradle, dreams lay bare.

Tales of creatures, kind and shy,
Fleeting glimpses, a fleeting sigh,
With every swish of the night's soft cloak,
A world awakens under the sky.

Beneath the hush, these shadows play,
In the cradle where the spirits sway,
They sing of love, of hope, of grace,
In the heart of night, forever stay.

Crescent Dreams Beneath Gnarled Branches

Crescent moons with silver seams,
Nestle down in woven dreams,
Beneath the gnarled, age-old limbs,
Where magic breathes and magic beams.

In whispers soft, the branches sway,
Cradling hopes where fairies play,
Dancing shadows, light and dark,
In the night, where secrets stay.

Each rustle tells a tale anew,
Of starlit skies and morning dew,
In the embrace of twilight's charm,
Life swirls in colors, wild and true.

The crescent cradles dreams unknown,
Within each heart, a seed is sown,
Beneath the bark of ancient trees,
The pulse of life, a timeless tone.

So linger long beneath the night,
Where shadows linger, worlds ignite,
In every sigh, a wish is made,
Beneath the stars, in pure delight.

Lullabies of the Midnight Grove

In the grove where shadows play,
Softly whispers drift away,
Lullabies of dawn unspoken,
In the heart, where dreams can stay.

The moonlight weaves a gentle thread,
Through every leaf, the fairies tread,
With every rustle, songs emerge,
In nature's cradle, softly spread.

Echoes ripple through the air,
As starlight flickers, bright and rare,
In the forest's hush, we find,
A melody beyond compare.

At midnight's peak, the world transforms,
Where beauty bursts, and magic swarms,
In the night, our spirits soar,
In the grove, the silence warms.

With every breath, the night enchants,
Each lullaby, a heartfelt dance,
Within the grove, our souls entwined,
In midnight's arms, we take our chance.

The Wane of Whispering Stars

In twilight's grip, the stars recede,
Their shimmering voices fade to a hush,
Once they sparkled, now they plead,
For dreams long lost, in the moon's blush.

With the night's breath, secrets wane,
Echoes dance on the whispering breeze,
In shadows deep, we hide our pain,
Finding solace in mystical trees.

Each heartbeat sings of tales untold,
Of love and loss in silver light,
As constellations weave threads of gold,
The universe cradles our silent fright.

Yet hope ignites in every sigh,
A flicker amidst the somber dusk,
Through the grief, the stars still lie,
A promise caught in their gentle husk.

So wander forth beneath the skies,
With eyes alight like fallen stars,
For in the dark, our spirit flies,
Carried by dreams, beyond our scars.

Arcane Murmurs of the Night Jewel

In the heart of night, a jewel gleams,
A whisper cloaked in shadows' embrace,
Its light uncovers forgotten dreams,
In fragile threads of time and space.

With every flicker, a story unfolds,
Of ancient magic and lost quests bright,
As starlit paths of wonder scrolled,
Beneath the cover of twilight's flight.

Murmurs of wisdom softly call,
A melody woven through eerie gloom,
Inviting brave hearts to rise or fall,
With promises of enchantment's bloom.

In this realm where shadows play,
The veil of night shall softly lift,
Each secret echo, a guiding ray,
Through murmurs shared, the spirits gift.

So chase the glow of the night jewel,
Let its essence seep into your soul,
For in its shine, we find the fuel,
To make our scattered stories whole.

Secrets Sold in a Glimmer of Light

In markets where the oddities gleam,
Secrets traded in whispers low,
A glimmering truth slips like a dream,
In shadows where the fragile go.

With every twinkle, a deal is struck,
Memories bartered, laughter sold,
In silence deep, we share our luck,
Holding close what darkness told.

Amidst the trinkets that glistening lie,
The heart's desires beckon and call,
In fleeting glimpses before they fly,
We grasp at moments, lest they fall.

For every secret holds a price,
An echo wrapped in emotion's thread,
In the glow of light, we pay that slice,
With every word that remains unsaid.

So seek the truth in the glimmer bright,
In the marketplace of the heart's might,
For within the shadows, lies delight,
And endless stories of the night.

Luminescent Visions of the Moonlit Shadow

Where moonlight drapes the world in silver,
Visions dance in a shadowed play,
They twirl and glide, an ethereal sliver,
In night's embrace, they find their way.

In every corner, dreams unfold,
Draped in mystery, they softly glide,
A tapestry of stories retold,
In the heart of darkness, they confide.

With each step taken upon the grass,
The whispers of night caress the air,
We follow the path where visions pass,
In the gentle glow, a lingering stare.

Through luminous realms, the magic flows,
In shadows deep, where wishes bloom,
The moon's soft light, a compass shows,
Guiding lost souls towards their room.

So revel in the visions bright,
Let their luminescence light your way,
For in the depths of the moonlit night,
Life's hidden wonders come out to play.

Nocturnal Lullabies of the Wicked

In shadows' arms, the whispers creep,
Where dreams entwine, and secrets sleep.
The nightingale sings, a mournful tune,
Beneath the watchful, gleaming moon.

Echoes twist through twisted trees,
Kisses of dusk, a bitter breeze.
With hearts enwrapped in midnight's thrall,
We dance with phantoms in the hall.

Cloaked in dark, the sorrows crawl,
As laughter rings, both near and far.
Where sorcery brews in cauldrons deep,
Nocturnal tales are meant to keep.

The cobwebbed path, the candle's glow,
Reveals the paths we dare not go.
With every step, the danger grows,
In tangled dreams, the wicked flows.

So listen close, oh wayward child,
To lullabies of the night, so wild.
For in the dark, the truth remains,
In wicked hearts, the magic reigns.

Hidden Language of the Celestial

Stars whisper softly, a language unseen,
In the canvas of skies, celestial sheen.
Constellations weave their tales divine,
In the silence of night, their stories align.

Moonbeams draw maps in the air so clear,
Each shimmer a note that only few hear.
With every twinkle, a secret unveiled,
Old cosmic riddles, in shadows, regaled.

Galaxies swirl in a dance of delight,
Their voices in symphony paint the night.
In the vastness, we find our place,
A hidden embrace, a timeless space.

Time bends around the twilit expanse,
Inviting the dreamers to join in the dance.
In whispered tones from the heavens above,
We find the language of hope and love.

So gaze upon stars with wonder anew,
Unlock their meanings, let them guide you.
For in the silence of shadows and light,
Lies the hidden language of the night.

Shimmering Lights of the Forbidden Grove

In the heart of the woods, where the wild ones play,
Shimmering lights beckon, leading astray.
With laughter of fae, the air comes alive,
In the forbidden grove, where spirits thrive.

Where blossoms of nightshade bloom in the dark,
And secrets are whispered by each little spark.
The path is a maze with enchantments entwined,
A dance of confusion, where fate's unconfined.

The glow of the will-o'-the-wisps draws you near,
With promises sweet and tinged with a fear.
As shadows uphold the ancient decree,
To wander here means to ask, to be free.

In the twilight, where both danger and delight,
Awaken the senses and blur day with night.
Each flicker a challenge, a riddle, a game,
For those who dare enter, never the same.

So heed the soft murmur of leaves as they sigh,
A warning, a spell, beneath the deep sky.
In shimmering lights, find both pleasure and pain,
In the forbidden grove, know the magic remains.

Wandering Spirits of the Endless Night

In the hush of the night, where the lost souls roam,
Wandering spirits seek their way home.
With whispers of sorrow, they drift on the breeze,
Carried by twilight through shadowed trees.

Each echo is filled with tales of despair,
Of love that once blazed now faded in air.
Lost destinies weave through the fabric of time,
Entwined in the rhythm of midnight's rhyme.

The withering moon, a guardian bold,
Watches these souls as their stories unfold.
With every step, they unravel the night,
In pursuit of the dawn, a flicker of light.

In the silence, their laughter brings joy and dread,
As memories linger for those who are dead.
They dance through the shadows, with grace so profound,

In the endless embrace of the night, they are found.

So if you should wander on these haunted trails,
Listen for whispers, for truth never fails.
For in the endless night, in darkness profound,
The wandering spirits, their solace profound.

Threads of Night in the Forest's Heart

In shadows deep, the secrets sigh,
Where ancient trees reach for the sky.
Moonlit paths weave tales of old,
Whispers of magic, daring and bold.

Among the roots, the stories grow,
Of faeries dancing, soft and low.
With every rustle, a promise made,
In the forest's heart, where dreams won't fade.

The nightingale sings a haunting tune,
Underneath the watchful moon.
Beneath the stars, the spirits play,
Guiding lost souls along their way.

In silver beams, the shadows twine,
Creating pathways, twinkling divine.
Through hidden glades, the wild things roam,
In the tangled wood, they find their home.

So venture forth, if you dare to tread,
Where the magic sleeps and fear is shed.
The forest calls, its voice sincere,
In the threads of night, let your heart steer.

Spells Cast Beneath the Enigmatic Sphere

Underneath the velvet sky,
The wizards gather, spells run high.
With whispered words, the candles glow,
As stars align in a timeless flow.

Bewitched by dreams and wishes spun,
In harmony, their powers run.
With potion brews and charms ablaze,
They dance through shadows, lost in haze.

In circles drawn, they join their fate,
Each incantation tears the gate.
The luminous sphere starts to glow,
Revealing truths only they know.

With every flick of wrist and wand,
The fabric of the night responds.
Mysteries unravel, fate aligns,
As ancient magic softly shines.

So heed the call, be brave and bold,
In worlds unseen, where dreams unfold.
Beneath the stars, where shadows steer,
Spells are cast in the mystic sphere.

Forbidden Whispers of the Celestial Labyrinth

In the labyrinth where shadows blend,
Forbidden whispers twist and bend.
With every turn, a secret waits,
Beyond the arch of ancients' gates.

Wanderers tread, their hearts aflame,
Searching for fortune, seeking fame.
But oh, beware the siren's call,
For truth may shatter, make one fall.

Hidden passages, a web of lies,
Entwined in echoes, lost in sighs.
With every step, the riddles gleam,
Reality fades into a dream.

The stars above seem to conspire,
Igniting the heart with sacred fire.
Through twists of fate, the brave they find,
The threads of destiny intertwined.

So linger not in fear or doubt,
For wisdom calls from paths without.
In the celestial maze, take flight,
And chase the whispers in the night.

Murmured Chants in the Forest of Elysium

In Elysium, where soft winds play,
Murmured chants greet the break of day.
With gentle voices, the trees conspire,
To weave a tapestry of desire.

Amidst the blooms, secrets arise,
In colors bright beneath the skies.
The woodland creatures join the song,
A harmony where all belong.

With every note, the spirit soars,
Through hidden glades and ancient doors.
In this haven, no shadows creep,
For light resides in every deep.

Each whispered prayer, a fragrant gift,
Lifting hearts, giving souls a lift.
In the forest corner, magic spills,
As laughter dances on the hills.

So join the throng and lose your fear,
In Elysium, all will draw near.
Let murmured chants lead you to grace,
In nature's arms, find your true place.

Secrets of the Flickering Stars

In the velvet of the night, they gleam,
Whispers hidden in cosmic dreams.
Twinkling secrets, old and wise,
Guiding hearts with their silent sighs.

A dance of light, they drift and spin,
Each flicker tells of where they've been.
A map of journeys, lost and found,
In every shimmer, magic's bound.

Beneath the veil of twilight's cloak,
The stars conspire, words unspoke.
With every blink, a tale unfolds,
Of love and loss, of brave and bold.

As dreams take flight on moonbeam trails,
The secrets weave through night's soft veils.
When shadows whisper, hearts will beat,
To the rhythm of a celestial greet.

For in the dark, where wonders play,
The flickering stars light up the way.
A promise kept in twinkling glow,
The magic lies in what we know.

A Gathering of Elusive Orbs

In twilight's hush, the orbs descend,
A gathering where dreams could blend.
Softly glowing, they pulse with light,
Each one carrying a wish tonight.

They dance on breezes, a delicate tease,
With laughter echoing among the trees.
In their presence, shadows fade,
Revealing secrets softly laid.

From distant lands, they found their way,
On moonlit paths where starlings play.
In colors bright, they twist and turn,
Holding stories for hearts to learn.

As twilight's song begins to swell,
The orbs weave tales, enchantment's spell.
In every flicker, hope takes flight,
A gentle touch of pure delight.

So linger close, and let them guide,
On this night where dreams abide.
For in their glow, we find the spark,
That lights the way through shadowed dark.

Mysteries Weaved in Midnight's Mist

In folds of mist, the night conceals,
A tapestry of whispered reels.
The moon unveils its silver thread,
Stitching dreams where fear has fled.

The air is thick with secrets spun,
Of worlds unseen, and battles won.
A wisp of smoke, a fleeting glance,
Invites the brave to take a chance.

With each soft step, the shadows breathe,
As magic weaves its silken wreath.
In every shimmer, tales untold,
Of forgotten hearts and valor bold.

Where silence reigns and echoes sleep,
The mysteries of the night we keep.
For in the dark, the light does bloom,
Chasing away the deepest gloom.

So step with care into the haze,
And let your spirit drift and gaze.
For in the mist, where wonders kiss,
We find the world's eternal bliss.

Fragments of the Moonlit Spell

Beneath the glow of silver light,
Fragments dance on this wondrous night.
Each glimmer holds a secret sigh,
A magic woven through the sky.

With whispered charms and gentle grace,
The moonlit spell finds its place.
In every flicker, a wish unfurls,
Woven dreams of distant worlds.

The air is thick with ancient lore,
Of times gone by, of myths and more.
A story wrapped in shadows deep,
Where timeless secrets softly seep.

As night extends its velvet hand,
We follow paths where starlight stands.
Each step a dance, each breath a chance,
In this enchanted moonlit trance.

So gather close, and hold the night,
For in the dark, there shines a light.
In fragments of the magic's pull,
We find our hearts forever full.

Guardians of the Embera Moonlight

In the hush of the night, they gather near,
Whispers of magic, they hold so dear.
Glistening stars in a velvet hue,
Wards of the ancients, the brave and true.

With wings so broad, they soar above,
Chasing shadows, they weave with love.
Crickets hum a soothing tune,
Beneath the watchful Embera moon.

Each flicker of light tells tales untold,
Of brave little hearts and spirits bold.
They guide the lost with silver beams,
As hope ignites through fluttering dreams.

Silent whispers brush against the trees,
As starlit sprites dance upon the breeze.
Guardians of night, with a gentle sway,
Keeping the darkness and fear at bay.

In the depths of the woods, secrets blend,
Around the corners where shadows bend.
From dusk till dawn, let their stories play,
For the guardians watch, come what may.

Intonations of the Nocturnal Voices

In the dark, a chorus raised,
Of creatures hidden, softly praised.
Bats take flight, with delicate grace,
Echoing dreams through time and space.

Hooting owls share wisdom of old,
While silver-moon beams, a sight to behold.
Whispers of twilight sway and sway,
As the night unfolds in a magical way.

Amidst the leaves, the stories flow,
Of ancient magic that few can know.
Beneath starlit skies, the night shall sing,
Voices of dusk, the joy they bring.

Each note a spell, each sound a thread,
Weaving a tapestry where dreams are spread.
With the dawn, the symphony fades,
But the echoes of night forever cascade.

In the heart of the forest, magic thrives,
In nocturnal tunes, the wonder derives.
Listen closely to the night's embrace,
For the voices of twilight, a timeless grace.

Chants from the Embered Shadows

In the dusk, shadows dance and play,
Where embers flicker, hearts lead the way.
Chants rise softly, rustling the leaves,
In the warmth of the night, the soul believes.

With every flicker, a story unfolds,
Of ancients who lit the dark with gold.
From the hearths of dreams, their memory glows,
A cycle of light that eternally flows.

Spirits entwined in the fiery glow,
Echoes of laughter from long ago.
Through whispered spells, their wisdom beckons,
Inviting all hearts to find their reckon.

The shadows of embers, a sanctuary bright,
Holding the secrets of day and night.
Here in the warmth, fears drift away,
As the chants from the shadows softly sway.

With the dawn, the embers will fade,
But the warmth of the night shall never jade.
In hearts eternal, the magic remains,
Within the embers, the spirit gains.

Glimmers of the Eldritch Heavens

Beyond the horizon, where legends reside,
Glimmers of twilight in dreams collide.
Stars interlace in an intricate dance,
Guiding the seekers with a mystic glance.

Through the cosmic canvas, colors unfold,
Stories of old in whispers retold.
Each shimmer a message from formless realms,
Awakening magic where spirit overwhelms.

Celestial whispers unfurl in the night,
Painting the darkness with ethereal light.
In the embrace of the cosmos, we find,
The dreams of the universe, intertwined.

Like constellations bright with flickering threads,
The hopes of the midnight softly spread.
Glimmers of wonder dart in the skies,
Lifting the hearts where true beauty lies.

As dawn approaches, and stars retreat,
Keep the glow within, a radiant beat.
For the heavens above will always share,
Their glimmers of magic, a love laid bare.

www.ingramcontent.com/pod-product-compliance
Ingram Content Group UK Ltd.
Pitfield, Milton Keynes, MK11 3LW, UK
UKHW021439290125
4349UKWH00039B/536